T0129851

What people are saying about …

PAUPER TO PRINCE

"Jesus made some incredible promises and he desires for them to be realized in your life. This exciting little book provides the wisdom you need to get you there. It's both a remarkable and refreshing read."

> – Pastor Arni Jacobson, Author, Former Green Bay Packers Chaplain, Former Mega-Church Pastor, and Grace International Executive (ArniJacobson.com)

"What's it like to be a man after God's own heart and to actually hear His voice? To walk with Him ever so closely? To brazenly throw it all away just to know Jesus more? What's it like to experience supernatural provision only for the season at hand or even just for a day? Read this little book and find out!"

> - Ryan Salzer, Operations Director of Milwaukee Wisconsin's JOY 1340 & 98.7 FM (Joy1340.com)

"In reading this book I feel like I'm playing that children's Chuck E Cheese game where the animals keep popping up and you get to knock 'em down as fast as you can. There's always another exciting surprise around the next page. It left me hungry for more. I can't wait until the next book comes out!"

> – Jodie Runchey, USA Team Outreach Coordinator of Promise Land Ranch School, Ghana, Africa, Inc. (PLRGhanaAfrica.com)

"'Pauper to Prince' provides life lessons for all of us. It substantiates the truths of the Bible through Pastor Paul's radical life journey of trusting in God's direction over one's own, regardless of where it leads. The book is very powerful."

– Jim and Sydney Drumel, Friends for Life Ministries

"I love Pastor Paul's 'voice' in this book! It is honest and real. It's an inspiring read that will have you saying, 'Oh yes, now I can see like never before how God has always been there for me.' If you need a fresh perspective in seeing just how God works in your life, then this book is for you."

– Vanessa Malo-Kurzinski, Equine-Assisted Coach, Therapist, and Psychologist of Foundations Farm (FoundationsFarm.com)

"This book conveys the good news message of Jesus in a way we can all relate to in our everyday lives. This is a must-read for encouragement in your walk with God. Following His lead in all you do can lead to excitement, joy, and a wonderful life in Jesus! Pastor Paul shares his life "by the seat of your pants" adventures so you too can trust in Him."

– Tara Essein, Co-Founder, Secretary, and Director of Promise Land Ranch School, Ghana, Africa, Inc. (PLRGhanaAfrica.com)

"Pastor Paul's testimony speaks of the Providence of God in the lives of those who commit themselves to Him. When one surrenders and becomes 'born again', one is adopted into God's family, and blessed with God becoming their Heavenly Father,

a Good Father who works out all the details of the life of his children."

"This little book tells a charming story of an ongoing miracle in the life of a pastor who simply said, 'Yes Lord. Come what may, I'll follow.' The book reminds me of the endearing truth found in Romans 8:28, '…we know that in all things God works for the good of those who love him, who have been called according to his purpose.' Everyone needs to read this!"

PAUPER TO PRINCE

PAUPER TO PRINCE

THE WILD JOURNEY OF A DISSATISFIED PASTOR WHO LEARNED THE SECRET TO HAVING IT ALL . . . AND HOW YOU CAN TOO

K PAUL BARTELME

"Every page is filled with heartwarming surprises
that take your breath away!"
Jodie Runchey, USA Team Outreach Coordinator, Promise Land Ranch, Ghana, Africa

authorHOUSE®

AuthorHouse™
1663 Liberty Drive
Bloomington, IN 47403
www.authorhouse.com
Phone: 1 (800) 839-8640

Edited by Mark Batten, Danica Bartelme,
Luke Bartelme, and www.Writers.Work.

Published by AuthorHouse 10/23/2018

ISBN: 978-1-5462-6474-3 (sc)
ISBN: 978-1-5462-6473-6 (e)

Print information available on the last page.

This book is printed on acid-free paper.

DOWNLOAD THE AUDIOBOOK FREE!

READ THIS FIRST

Just to say thanks for buying my book, I would like to give you the audiobook version 100% FREE!

TO DOWNLOAD, GO TO:

https://kpaulbartelme.com/free-download/

Enter the password: Becomeaprince777

Enjoy!

ATTENTION!

Half of the proceeds of this book is going
to Promise Land Ranch School!

What's that? PLR is Ghana Africa's first non-
profit private Kindergarten-12th grade school that
provides an exceptional quality and free Christ-
centered education to the poorest of the poor, not to
mention meeting their felt needs such as food, clean
water, clothing, etc. As of 2018, the school has three
hundred students and growing! Their vision is to
raise up the next generation of leaders in the Body of
Christ who will transform that region of the world.

And we get to be a part of that!

As Christians, we're not only obligated to
make a difference in our community but
also beyond. Way beyond. Even "to the ends
of the earth", to borrow Jesus' words.

So, what are you waiting for?
Buy the book already… and bless a child today.

After buying the book, go check out the school at https://www.plrghanaafrica.com/ and sponsor a child. That's going to feel awesome.

Promise Land Ranch School Ghana, Africa
Transformation through Education

This book is dedicated to the numerous
Milwaukeeans who told me that I needed
to write a book after telling them my story.

%

A heartfelt "thank you" to my amazing wife
Danica and our kiddos for being such good
sports. "Wow, what a ride, huh?!"

%

A heartfelt "thank you" to my Dad whose blessings
for my family have multiplied. They've been
poured out onto my extended church family, the
greater Milwaukee area (through the church's
past radio broadcast ministry), and even to
the ends of the earth (through this book).

%

A heartfelt "thank you" to my "Bonus" Dad and
Mom for all the many blessings throughout my
life. I love you unconditionally and always will.

%

To the congregation and staff of New Vintage Church:
"Fasten your seatbelts 'cause we're just gettin' started!"

The headline from Milwaukee's newspaper *The Christian Courier* read, "Pastor from San Diego, CA Pulls Up Stakes and Moves to West Allis, WI."

The article began with the following words:

The conversation goes like this: "Nice to meet you. Where'd you move from?" "San Diego, California." Without fail, the reaction is, "WHAT? AND YOU MOVED HERE?!"

At this point in the conversation I would begin sharing how my family and I ended up in West Allis. And I'm excited to share with you as well because everyone says that the story is wild.

But don't take my word for it. Find out for yourself.

CONTENTS

Chapter 5: To Infinity And Beyond   35

- The Season Of Transition
- Preparing for Takeoff
- 3... 2... 1... Annnnd Takeoff
- On Mission
- Where We're at and Where We're Going

CHAPTER 1

THE LETTER THAT CHANGED EVERYTHING

"God makes all things beautiful in its time."

~ King Solomon ~

The Letter

(Fall of 2015)

We were living in Escondido, California, a city about ½ hour north of San Diego. There was this letter that had been sitting in the don't-need-to-open-right-away pile on the dining room table that was peculiar because of its return address.

I asked Danica, "Do you know anyone from Illinois?"

She replied, "Nope." Intriguing. I grabbed the letter, opened it, and sat down to read it.

The contents comprised of an attractive-looking family studio portrait and a note. As I began reading it, I was having a hard time deciphering what was being communicated. This lady in her mid-to-late 30's claimed that I was her half-brother! Her dad told her around twelve years ago that she had one out there somewhere in the world from a previous marriage. She wanted to find me, and she was happy to locate my home address. She told me that it was important to stay on top of my regular doctor check-ups due to having a history of heart disease. She expressed a desire to develop a sibling relationship, yet if I thought it was too weird a thing to pursue, then she would understand. I couldn't make heads or tails of it all, so I gave the note to Danica.

"Umm, what is this lady trying to say to me exactly?"

Danica replied rather slowly and timidly, "She's saying that Joe isn't your biological father."

My half-sister wrote the letter assuming, and understandably so, that my parents would have told me that my dad adopted me. But they didn't. The blaring question at this point has been, "Well, why not?"

Why Didn't My Parents Tell Me?

The answer to the question remains a mystery. And that's okay with me. A common reply to such a statement has been, "How could that be okay with you? You're accepting of that?" Sure. I mean, one could speculate as to why. Yet at the end of the day, the wisest thing to conclude is that they thought it was most beneficial for me not to know. They had good intentions in mind always.

God is so amazing. He is faithful to "make all things beautiful in its time," to borrow the ancient words of King Solomon in his book Ecclesiastes. Yet, the promise is conditional. If you were to follow Jesus unequivocally, then you can take that promise to the bank. On the other hand, if you were *not* to follow Jesus, then I don't really understand how one can have the confidence that the promise will eventually come to pass.

So, when I say that I was okay with not understanding why my parents didn't tell me that I was adopted, then… yes, I was okay with that. God had taught me the lessons I needed to learn to be set free from unforgiveness prior to opening the letter.

Another question that is asked is, "But you had to know that there was something askew in your growing-up years, right?"

We Create Our Own Reality

Sure, the clues were there, and there were times when I inquired, yet the issue was swept under the rug. Finally, there was a point in my life when I shrugged my shoulders and resorted to accepting the "fact" that Joe is my biological father. And life went on.

See, I have this uncanny ability to create my own reality. And so do you. It's part of what makes us human. We're subjective beings and we create our own realities to cope with life the best way we know how.

Here's the thing: There's our reality and then there's reality-reality. Reality-reality just might be too painful to accept, at least until the opportune time. So, we create our own reality. The thing about this though, is that our reality isn't real, or true. And reality-reality has a way of coming to the surface and displaying to the world the truth of the matter.

This reminds me of Jesus' words in the Gospel of Luke, "… there is nothing hidden that will not be disclosed, and nothing concealed that will not be known or brought out into the open." Yep, you can count on reality, sooner or later, rearing its ugly head and forcing you to make a decision: Are you going to deal with whatever it is that has been brought out into the open or not? This is called *mercy*.

Mercy! Reality-reality is God's mercy on display. He

earnestly desires for "mercy to triumph over judgment", as the book of James in the Bible teaches us, yet this is on you and me. We get to decide. (Perhaps reality-reality's head isn't so ugly after all.)

God loves us so much that He will give us opportunities to deal with our baggage before it's too late. One way or the other, it's going to be dealt with. The question is, "Would you like to deal with it on this side of eternity or on the other side?"

I don't know about you, but I'd rather travel to the other side luggage-free. No need to check in any luggage and no need for a carry-on either, no sir.

Ever since I opened that letter, reality-reality's head has been far from ugly. On the contrary, with all the recent developments it has been beautiful. Reality-reality can be beautiful for you too because, according to the Bible, God doesn't play favorites. What He's done for me He desires to do for you as well because "He works all things together for good unto those who love Him…" and, well, the ancient wisdom from King Solomon also applies here; "He makes all things beautiful in its time."

He makes all things beautiful in its time. Is that a reality in your life? It can be.

One of the many beautiful realities in my life is that I acquired a whole new family, most notably a crazy-amazing half-sister.

My Sister from the Same Mister

So, back to the story. If you recall, my sister had expressed a desire to develop a sibling relationship.

After spending a few days re-configuring my family relationships and re-calibrating my life, I sent her an email and we hit it off like old friends. Thus began a flurry of deep, meaningful phone conversations and emails.

Vanessa and I talked about all kinds of stuff: What our families were like growing up, our passions, fears, careers, latest movies we watched, how we met our spouses, how we came up with our children's names, what we liked to do for fun… We even discussed such things that aren't supposed to be talked about in polite company if you'd like company to remain polite. You know, the trinity of religion, money, and politics. It seemed that nothing was off the table.

We emailed each other pictures too. Vanessa sent some cool ones of my biological father Ken's factories along with newspaper articles and such. There was one picture that I'll never forget.

It was a picture of Ken when he was a boy around four years old. He had a sailor outfit on and he looked exactly like my youngest son Luke when he was the same age. When I saw that picture on my computer screen, I enlarged it and then brought Danica into my home office.

I told her, "Wow, what a great outfit Luke had on back then, huh?" (At this time Luke was nine years old.)

She replied, "That is a great outfit. So cute. But, umm, I don't remember him having an outfit like that. Weird."

"Yes, that is weird… because *that's not Luke!*"

She was stunned. "What?"

"That's Ken!"

It was only fitting to bring the kiddos into the office now and see if they would fall for the prank too… and they did.

And then…

There was the day that I received an email from Vanessa telling me that her and her family would be vacationing in Southern California and wanted to visit. Somebody pinch me.

CHAPTER 2
THE POST-LETTER ADVENTURE

"You will know the truth and the truth will set you free."

~ Jesus ~

The Kurzinski Family Visit

(February of 2016)

Well, the day finally came, the day that Vanessa, her husband Mark, and their super-cute kiddos came to visit. Mark has relatives on the West Coast and they vacation regularly out here, so why not include the long-lost half-brother and his family in the itinerary?

We met up at a local restaurant and had lunch together. Jake, Lily, and Lukey were in school at the time, so it was just Danica and myself. After all that we learned about each other through our correspondence, it was awesome to be sitting at a table opposite of one another. Mark and Vanessa made an impressive team as they gracefully helped their toddlers Nikki and Lucas with their food while they ate and conversed. And then Vanessa pulled out a nicely-wrapped box and gave it to me.

"I got you a present," she said.

I opened it and pulled out a DNA test kit from AncestryDNA.com. I was surprised… in a good way.

"Well, you want to be sure, right?"

"Sure, yes, of course," I replied.

In the months that passed since I opened her letter, I hadn't thought of taking a DNA test to confirm Vanessa's claim. Deep down inside I just knew. Clues in the form of memories had floated to the surface and that was all the confirmation I needed. Yet, it just made sense to take the test and put an end to the controversy once and for all.

Ah, to do such would usher in a whole new season and allow God the opportunity to perform a work of redemption – of freedom - for everyone involved. (As a disciple of Jesus, this is ultimately all that I live for.) What do I mean by this?

God's all about *freedom*. He came to our sin-drenched world to set the captives (everyone) free. That's His modus operandi in a statement, to set the captives free. And He's still in the business of doing so. But how?

Well, one way is by shaking up the status-quo in one's life. It's only by doing so that one can re-evaluate their paradigm. The Holy Spirit's voice then has the opportunity to be heard. And, I cringe to write this, but in most instances the situation must bring a level of discomfort that exceeds the level of discomfort to surrender. To finally surrender to that *Voice*. The Voice of freedom.

"You will know the truth, and the truth will set you free." – Jesus in John chapter 10

Well, free from what?

From past hurts. From destructive habits and hang-ups. From unforgiveness, bitterness, and resentment. From depression, despair, and hopelessness. In other words, from all the adverse effects of sin.

He sets us free so we can experience *restoration* in our relationships, our health, and every other area in our lives. He earnestly desires that we experience a peace that passes all understanding, a hope made alive, and an indescribably glorious joy!

This, my friend, is *true* Christianity and it's possible by the grace of God enabling us to activate our faith in Jesus; a faith so dynamic that it leads to a life of freedom.

So, bring it, Holy Spirit. Shake up the status-quo.

Back to my story.

Lunch with the Kurzinskis was wonderful. They also accepted myself and Danica's invitation to come to church with us that Sunday, the church I was pastoring at the time, of course. And a good time was had by all.

Then the time came for them to leave for the airport. As Mark was piling their luggage into the car, Vanessa approached me in our driveway and said, "I just got off the phone with Ken, and he would like to meet you and your family. He would like to invite you to spend this summer's vacation with him and the Malo clan in the Chicago area."

The pleasant surprises throughout this season was not lacking. "Well, that's great. We don't currently have any summer plans, so sure."

My matter-of-fact reply didn't accurately convey the excitement that I felt inside. My family was offered the opportunity to meet my biological father and Danica's father-in-law. Jake, Lily, and Lukey's grandfather! There was only one thing holding us back.

"Vanessa, you're aware that my family is not your typical middle-class American family. We don't live for extravagant vacations and such. We could, but we don't. We're more likened to a missionary family. Every bit of financial resource from our church and side businesses is expended on our mission. Not to mention that where we live is expensive, so much so that most pastors are bi-vocational and/or their spouses work. That said, we don't have the financial means to fly a family out to vacation at Chicago."

"Oh, that's all I needed to hear," was her reply. "I'll just have Dad write you a check."

Danica and I were stunned. And like the virgin Mary when she found out the news about her baby boy, we also had things to ponder in our hearts.

We ended up accepting Ken's offer. What an adventure.

The Start to a Most Memorable Vacation

(Summer of 2016)

A few weeks after the Kurzinski visit, I received a letter from Ken. It was a surreal moment as I studied his handwriting and gracious words. Included in the letter was a check that included not only the means for the vacation, but also the means for a good start on the kids' college funds.

I had the opportunity to back out of this whole thing, yet I knew that God's fingerprints were all over this. I didn't even give it a thought to the contrary because I have been walking intimately with God for so many years and I could hear His voice saying, "This is the path. Walk in it." (Not to mention that by this time Vanessa had shared lots of details with me about Ken.)

Summer came, and then the day came when we drove

to the airport, destination "Windy City". We learned that Vanessa is quite the talented vacation planner and host. Everything was scheduled out, which comprised of not only the usual tourist spots but also the meeting where she would be introducing me to Ken.

I'll never forget the day I met him. Danica and I were sitting in the rental car at the parking lot outside of his coffee house.

I turned to her and said, "Well, this is surreal. But, you know what? I feel great. Ultimately, it doesn't really matter if I like him or not, or if he likes me or not. Would be nice if we liked each other though."

"Aww, babe, what's not to like?" was Danica's reply.

"I don't have the time to answer that right now," I said with a wry smile as I got out of the car.

"See you later, and… well, have fun!" Danica shouted out the window as she drove away.

The Meet Up

The experience walking into the coffee house was not unlike walking into a Starbucks. I noticed Vanessa sitting at a table in the back of the main room and made a beeline toward her as I walked past the sound of the expresso machines and conversational chatter.

"Ken will be here any minute. How's it going? Nervous?"

"Strangely, not as nervous as I thought I'd be."

We ordered a bite and some beverages. Right around the time we got resettled in our chairs, Ken walked into the room. As soon as he noticed us, he smiled big and waved as he made his way over. I got up and began walking toward him with a big smile on my face too.

We reached out our hands for a handshake and, as is Ken's custom, the handshake accommodated a light hug.

The conversation was informal and pleasant. Even joyful. There was no weirdness; rather, we felt free to talk about whatever came to mind. (As I type this, I'm reminded of Jesus' words, "Whom the Son sets free will be free indeed.") One of the things that Ken shared was the experience he had when he saw me as a baby.

My mom came to visit him at the machine shop he just opened. She had me in a stroller and said something to the effect of, "Well, I thought you might like to see your baby." It was a well-intended gesture.

Ken reached down to take a good look. (Little did he know that it would be his last look for forty-six years.) I wrapped my teeny-tiny little fingers around his index finger. He engaged in a bit of small talk with my Mom and then said, "Well, I need to get back to work." He had those machines running day and night. And he had a different vision for his future than what my mom had, so off they went on their separate ways.

(Don't get me wrong. One of Ken's heart's desires was to have a family. It's just that a man is wired differently than a woman, of course. He was engrossed in building a future of stability, and even prosperity, for his family. And my Mom profoundly needed something else that he couldn't provide at the time.)

As it was when I first met Vanessa, Ken and I hit it off like old friends. Deep, meaningful conversations were had as he took me on scenic drives throughout the region. He shared about his growing-up years, how he met my Mom, the houses he lived in, the factories he built, my grandparents, and many other things as well.

There was one thing he shared that made the biggest impression of all and radically changed the course of my family's future as well as my pastoral career.

The Offer

It was the 4th of July 2016, the day of myself and Danica's 22nd wedding anniversary. Yep, I lost my independence on Independence Day, ha-ha.

We were having a fantastic time on our vacation and it was arranged for us to celebrate the holiday at Ken's house in Barrington Hills. Danica and I were sitting on a couch in the living room by ourselves as we gazed out the sliding glass doors to watch the kiddos play in the swimming pool. Ken walked into the room and approached us.

"Well, there you two love birds are. Hey, there's something I'd like to talk with you about."

"What's that?" was my reply.

"I don't know exactly how to say it, so I'll be blunt. I'd love to purchase a church property outright and donate it to your non-profit."

Needless to say, we were stunned. And before I knew it, the following words just kind of fell out of my mouth. "Sure, we'd be open to that."

"Great! Once you get back home, you and Vanessa can start looking for a property that fits the criteria necessary to grow a church. We'll start with the closest radius to Chicago and keep expanding from there."

Now, the blaring question in your mind at this moment might be, "Why would we be open to that?" To answer that question, we'll need to rewind back twelve years.

CHAPTER 3
SO MUCH MORE TO BE HAD

Jesus + Nothing = Everything

~ Tullian Tchividjian ~

Life was Awesome… and Yet…

(Summer of 2004)

Danica and I owned a little house a dozen blocks from the beach in Oceanside, California with the pristine yard, a white picket fence, and a cat named Chloe. Danica loved her career as a hair stylist and I was on paid staff as an associate preaching pastor. I had a music lesson/artist development business which complemented ministry nicely due to being full-time pay on part-time hours. I just finished producing a recording of a Christian rock band which I planned on shopping around to the labels. Lol, I remember Danica breastfeeding Jacob while tracking vocals.

Life was awesome.

And yet deep down inside, I knew that there was so much more to be had. God gave me the desire to pursue greater heights in ministry.

It finally came to a point where I had to share with Danica the vision: I believed God wanted us to sell the house, put in notice at work, close the businesses, pay off our debt, and move to only-God-knows-where to plant a church. (I won't bore you with all the other details; i.e. the way that God was engineering the circumstances to prepare for this new season.)

As you can imagine, she wasn't receptive to the vision.

The Planet We're From

Not only was Danica not receptive to the vision… she thought I was crazy. She wasn't alone. My decision rattled many people because it didn't fit into their brand of cultural Christianity. They couldn't understand why God would instruct me to do such a thing. Yet, the very reason why He did was because I prayed to Him long ago, "Lord, my life is Yours. Do with it what You will." That remained my mindset throughout my time in Bible College as well as my years in ministry.

Reminds me of that ol' Glen Kaiser song, "Surrender":

Lord and Savior, we have nothing without You
There is nothing we can do
But to serve and follow You

And surrender, to surrender, all our dreams
All we are, all that we are to become, all our love

Anyway, many were baffled. I even had a friend ask me, "Really, you're going to do this? What planet are you from?"

His question made sense. Why not just settle for what we have? Coast through the years and decades, keep growing that retirement nest egg, and pay off the mortgage? Enjoy our grandbabies, grow old and die?

Because that's not what Biblical Christianity is all about. There's so much more to be had than settling and coasting.

There are so many – perhaps the majority of

America – who call themselves Christians and yet are not experiencing the promises of God being realized in their lives. Promises like living a prosperous life in every way. No longer being bound up in any form of fear, anxiety, and worry. Protection from unnecessary suffering due to seeing life through the lens of the Bible.

In other words, living out Jesus' audacious claim of making available a life filled to overflowing with peace and joy, purpose and meaning. A life that He claimed only He can provide.

The reason why many are not experiencing these promises being realized is because they're conditional, and they'll be realized by becoming a disciple of Jesus, not just a believer in Him.

That said, is it possible for such things to be a reality in one's life without having to pursue a vision like mine that comprised of so much sacrifice? Absolutely. Yet, a question worth pondering is this: Would you be willing to pursue such a vision if He asked you to?

This reminds me of an interesting formula I came across years ago:

Jesus + Nothing = Everything

Get that and you're good-to-go.

Anyway, back to my story.

Soon enough, God confirmed in Danica's heart our calling. We had no idea where we were moving, whether it would be to a neighboring town or across the country. We felt like Abraham who heard God's voice to go to a place where he would later receive his inheritance.

Abraham by faith obeyed and went out even though he didn't know where he would end up.

(September of 2004)

We ended up in Escondido which is about 15 miles east of Oceanside. At our new home my favorite place to cry was in the shower. What need was there to cry? The transition was going smooth for the family and we had successfully planted our first church. Why the tears?

I Was Dying

I'll explain.

I still held out hope that some of my clients' music recordings, of which I owned half of the song-writing credits to, would generate more and more radio airplay and eventually make the national stage.

I never knew that this part of my life was NOT under God's control. This part of me was dying and it was painful. I didn't realize how much space in my head was rented out to all the song lyrics, melodies and guitar riffs. Even after the big move, I was still programmed to be, alongside a husband, father, and minister... a songwriter/producer. I didn't think there was anything wrong with this because, well, it was partly how I paid the mortgage at the time.

Like slowly turning down the volume of a high fidelity stereo system, the music faded away and more space in my head was made available for God's voice. The songwriter/producer part of me died.

The point is this: Whatever it is that you hold out hope for… Whatever you try to derive ultimate satisfaction from, well, that's your idol that you serve by sacrificing your money and time to. And wherever your money and time goes, your heart follows. "Wherever your treasure is, there your heart will be also," to borrow Jesus' words.

It could be the pursuit of true love or it could be to retire comfortably. It could be something expensive and shiny or it could be a job title. It could be a Christian ministry. The examples outnumber the stars in the sky. In the words of Bob Dylan, "You're gonna have to serve somebody, yes indeed…"

These things are not inherently bad or wrong to pursue. What's wrong is when they become the source of where you believe ultimate satisfaction is derived from.

Well then, is there a source from where you can experience *ultimate satisfaction*? The answer is yes, and that source is found in none other than Jesus. He Himself made that claim in the form of an analogy. He claimed that He is the source of *living water* and that if you drink it you would never thirst again! You would, sooner or later, be completely satisfied in Him and in Him alone.

Also, this living water would become in you "a spring of water welling up to eternal life", as the Gospel of John states. Eternal life, by the way, is lived in the here and now, not just after you die and go to heaven. Eternal life IS ultimate satisfaction, among other things.

The crazy thing about deriving satisfaction from Jesus is that you don't have to do anything to try and earn it. You can't. Rather, just believe with a faith that is so dynamic that it leads to the desire to follow him obediently. How do you do that? Well, the answer is found in your Bible if you have one. If you don't, then get one. Doing so would prove to yourself that you are finally over and done with traveling down the "dead-end streets (where) every time I thought I'd got it made, it seemed the taste was not so sweet," to borrow the words of David Bowie from his song "Changes".

A New Chapter Had Begun

So yes, to summarize, a new chapter in our lives had begun and the words of the ancient prophet Isaiah had never rung truer; "See, I am doing a new thing! Now it springs up… I am making a way in the wilderness and streams in the wasteland… to give drink to my people… that they may proclaim my praise."

This new chapter comprised of twelve long, hard, and sometimes brutal years… and yet I wouldn't have wished them to be different. Really? Why?

Because those promises I mentioned earlier became a reality in my life.

I honestly thought they were realized during the eleven years prior in ministry. Yet, little did I know that there was so much more to be had.

CHAPTER 4

A STORM WAS A BREWIN'

"Do your best, pray that it's blessed, and let God do the rest. By doing so, you can smilingly wash your hands of the consequences."

~ Keith Green / Oswald Chambers ~

One of my goals in writing this book is that it would have a conversational tone about it. I'm hoping that it's easy for you to imagine us sitting across from one another in a coffee house and you're enjoying your favorite beverage while I tell you my story.

Another one of my goals is to only share details that are directly related to the big move that my family and I made from Southern California to the Midwest. That said, the following details comprise a few sparse highlights from 2004 to 2014.

Life was Awesome... Again

(2004-2014)

Danica and I had enjoyed "cultivating faithfulness in the land" (to borrow the ancient psalmist's words) for quite some time now as we labored together in our little church. It was a lovely church and it felt like family, yet it just wasn't the Lord's will for it to grow significantly.

There were different reasons for this; most notably, our sanctuary was too small to accommodate significant growth. As the saying goes, a fish can only grow as big as the fishbowl will allow. We tried different things. We knocked on various doors of opportunity, yet God never opened any to rectify the situation, and that was okay with us because we were happy and content serving in whatever capacity He had us serve in.

Content though I was, God had given me a desire to make a greater impact than what most small-to-mid-sized churches typically make. I was full, yet hungry for transformation both in the community and at-large.

So, the doors that He *did* open were opportunities I never thought to pursue. I accepted an offer to write a weekly column in one of the city's newspapers with a circulation of tens of thousands. I began uploading my sermons onto a website that made them available to the public and developed a weekly listenership of thousands. I was, and still am, a founding member on the advisory board that oversees the development of Ghana, Africa's first non-profit Christian elementary school. "Promise Land Ranch" provides free education to the poorest of the poor, not to mention meeting their felt needs. Three hundred students and growing! Their vision is to raise up the next generation of Christian leaders in that region of the world. Check them out at www.PLRGhanaAfrica.com and consider sponsoring a child.

There was yet another door that the Lord opened early on in my senior pastoral career. I was blessed with the opportunity to transfer my ordainment certificate to Grace International, which is a growing fellowship of churches comprising of 3,600+ congregations in 107 countries. I have now been blessed to fellowship with pastors from two different USA districts and I cannot recommend the organization enough. Check them out at www.GraceChurches.tv.

In addition to ministry, Danica and I had two more children, Lily and Luke. We were all happy and healthy. We moved into a nice neighborhood and the kiddos were in great schools. In fact, I started teaching music on the side again and that was something the Lord blessed big-time. Before I knew it, the business had grown to 50+ instructors over an 8-year period providing private music lessons in four counties.

The church and business made for a great marriage, not unlike a church and children's day care center in many ways. Our sanctuary served also as a performance hall and the children's church rooms as music lesson rooms. There were separate lobbies for both entities. It was a pretty sweet arrangement.

Yep, life was awesome again. Little did I know that a storm was a brewin'.

A Storm was a Brewin'

I had an employee who was a talented internet marketer/account manager and consequently the business grew fast. Too fast. I had taken the proper measures to prepare for any possible repercussions for this, but it was too little, too late. My employee's time had eventually run its course and he put in a two-week notice.

No problem. Time to start interviewing a replacement. Little did I know that things were not going to turn around.

After multiple interviews over the course of several months a replacement was never hired. The business started to shrink. And shrink more.

This was around the time that the management company for our building informed me that the owner was planning on nearly doubling my payment when my lease contract expires. Danica and I responded by raising the sub-lease payments on our two tenants which would have rectified the situation. They ended up putting in their thirty-day notice!

The Spiral Downward

So, I'm wondering, "Lord, what's going on? Did I do something wrong?"

His reply was, "No, you didn't do anything wrong. Just trust in Me. Trust in Me with all your heart and lean not on your own understanding. I have a sovereign plan and it's for your good, so I'll navigate you through this. Don't fret! Rather, just enjoy My presence and flow to the rhythms of My grace."

Easier said than done. But hey, it's possible. If *you* happen to be in a season of a downward spiral, you will want to look back with a smile.

A smile. That reminds me…

There are two quotes that I tied together long ago that provided all the wisdom I needed during that season.

The first quote is from Keith Green, contemporary Christian pianist, singer, and songwriter. It's a refrain from one of his songs and it goes like this, "Do your best, pray that it's blessed, and let God do the rest." The second quote is from Oswald Chambers; "…smilingly wash your hands of the consequences."

Put these two together and it flows like this:

"Do your best, pray that it's blessed, and let God do the rest.

By doing so, you can smilingly wash
your hands of the consequences."

Think about that for a moment. God calls me to give my all in bettering the situation as I pray, seeking His guidance and direction. That's my responsibility.

The next part is challenging. I need to trust that whatever is out of my control is in His control. No fretting allowed.

Okay, so if I'm living up to my responsibility and I'm also trusting that He will live up to His, which is to prosper me and not to harm me, to give me a hope and a future… then I can *smilingly* wash my hands of the consequences.

I can smile throughout the whole ordeal!

However it turns out will be according to God's sovereign will. (It may not turn out quite the way I'd like it to though. Rarely does. And I've learned to be okay with that.)

What I'm saying is that God is behind the scenes working out all the details… and it's all for my good. His words, not mine. How can I be confident in this? Because I love Him and am called according to His purpose. Again, His words, not mine.

How freeing is that?

(Spring of 2014)

So anyway, back to my story.

God had a new facility ready for my remaining instructors and one for the church too, a public-school gymnasium. Regarding the church, wow, we were in for a new season of what could be best described as the "wilderness wanderings".

If you grew up in Sunday school, you're probably familiar with that phrase. It's derived from a story in the Old Testament.

When the Israelites were liberated from Egyptian bondage, the Lord directed them into the wilderness for forty years where they were taught some profound lessons and their faith was tested. A new generation rose up with the great expectancy that the Lord's promise to Abraham would be realized; they would eventually end up in the "land flowing with milk and honey" where they would make their permanent residence and become a great nation and a great blessing to the world.

So yes, we became what is called a mobile church. We had to haul our gear from the garage to the school and back every Sunday. What an experience. Yet, we didn't let it steal our joy. We had a great expectancy that the Lord would usher in a new season out of the wilderness and into a permanent residence ourselves.

So, we lugged our gear to a most undesirable location. And there were some Sundays when the school was unavailable, so we would have church in the park. And then, thank God, our lease expired. We signed a new lease at a banquet hall which unfortunately did not have adequate storage onsite for us. And there were more Sundays of unavailability. As you can imagine, our little church got littler. And so did the business.

Again, I found myself wondering, "Lord, what's going on?" It was around that time that I noticed Vanessa's letter sitting on the dining room table.

CHAPTER 5
TO INFINITY AND BEYOND

A man's heart plans his way, but the Lord directs his steps."

~ King Solomon ~

The Season Of Transition

(Summer of 2016)

We just got home from vacationing in Chicago and I was excited to get to work researching church properties that would meet our qualifications. I started with a tight radius around the city and kept expanding from there. And I kept expanding more. Due to the scarcity of options, the radius expanded out to 150 miles.

There were a couple of properties that warranted a personal visit, yet for some reason or another, they didn't work out. The weeks were flying by… and (gulp) winter was approaching.

Being a So-Cal family, we weren't too thrilled about the prospect of moving to the Midwest in the dead of winter. On the contrary, we were about ready to postpone the whole deal until I got a call from Vanessa.

"Paul, check it out. Our realtor just called with some great news. He was driving through West Allis, Wisconsin to show a property and noticed a "for sale" sign in front of a church. So, he pulls over and ends up talking with the owner who just put the property up for sale a few days ago. Check it out online. The address is…"

"Wow, okay. But even if this property meets our qualifications, we're looking at moving around December or January. I can't even watch the weather on the national news anymore."

Her immediate reply had a healthy dose of laughter. "And your point is? From what I know about you, Paul, I thought you wouldn't want it any other way!"

"Ha-ha, yep, you do have a good point there. Bring it!"

After getting off the phone, I hopped on the internet to check out this town named West Allis in Wisconsin. Turns out that it's just outside the city of Milwaukee. Milwaukee is where the Bartelme clan lives, you know, my step-dad's side of the family. Holy cow, I not only get to live close to my newly-found family on my dad's side, but also the family I've always known on my step-dad's side!

"God moves in mysterious ways," as the 19th century hymn lyric written by William Cowper states. Indeed, He sure does. This made for some very interesting times.

Preparing for Takeoff

(November of 2016)

The church property was purchased in November which brought us to the point of no return. There was a lot to take care of in a short amount of time. We had a music lesson business to dissolve which comprised of our winter music recital. We had a church entity to dissolve which comprised of remaining church services and activities. We had a big sending-off party, and a lot of packing to do as well. Oh yes, and Christmas. Can't forget Christmas.

The hustle and bustle of the holidays is a stressful time for most. It goes without saying that this one was extraordinarily challenging for the Bartelme family, especially for our oldest, Jake. He was thirteen at the time.

There was one evening when Danica walked Jake into my office. The poor kiddo was crying. His life in So-Cal was awesome. He had close friends, went to a fantastic school, and excelled in music and academia.

"I'm so sorry, Jake. I wish it could have worked out here. It just wasn't the Lord's will. You can trust that He has some great friends waiting for you in West Allis. And you can stay in touch with your friends here too, right?"

"But why do we have to leave?" he asked in between sniffles.

"Jake, this not an uncommon thing to do. Families move all the time all over the country for various reasons."

I continued, "Oftentimes we don't understand why things don't work out the way we'd like them to. This is why it's called a 'faith-walk'. Yet we can trust that our Heavenly Father knows best, right? And where He guides, He provides. The well of provision has simply run dry here and the Lord has a new Kingdom Assignment, a new mission for us to carry out."

Jake walked over to my library as I was talking and picked up one of my parishioner's gifts that was sitting on a shelf. It was a plastic toy soldier from the son of a Marine Corps officer.

Jake turned towards me with that soldier in his hand and said, "This is you, isn't it? Kind of like Ayden's dad. You're one of God's soldiers and when He has a new assignment for you, then you have to carry it out."

"That's right, except our battlefield is spiritual and

Ayden can't go with his dad when he's deployed. Think about that."

"You're a soldier too, Jake. Think about all that you did for the church. The apostle Paul wrote to his protégé Timothy that one should be careful not to get too tangled up in civilian affairs but rather to please his commanding officer. Well, Paul was referring to our relationship with Jesus. He's our Commanding Officer and we're His soldiers. The new Kingdom Assignment He has for us is so awesome. You choose to believe that, Jake, and you're good-to-go. You thank God for the awesome season that is upon us and you celebrate it. Okay?"

"Okay, I'll do my best, Dad." Good ol' Jake. He gave me a hug and left my office with a determined smile.

Regarding the church, we spent a lot of time discussing, praying and discerning what the Lord's will was going to be: Morph it into a campus church under our new church headquarters in Wisconsin? Managing that would be too much work under the circumstances. Turn it over to an associate? Out of those who had what it took, they didn't meet the Biblical qualifications. Assist in merging with another church? We didn't know of another church that had just the right DNA for a successful merge. So, we ended up encouraging our parishioners to get plugged into other churches in the area and followed up with them to ensure a smooth transition.

Then came the end of a twelve-year chapter of myself and Danica's lives in a senior pastoral capacity. Twelve years behind us and eight days on the road ahead of us.

3... 2... 1... Annnnd Takeoff

(January of 2017)

We were blessed to have lots of friends help us load up the largest U-Haul moving van available, as well as the largest enclosed trailer.

Danica, Jake, Luke, our cat Heidi, and our dog Zoe piled into our roomy mini-van, which towed an open trailer that toted all our personal luggage along with my Harley-Davidson motorcycle. (Living in the mildest climate in America, what need did we have for a second car?)

Lily kept me company in the cabin of the U-Haul and down the road we went with one last wave goodbye to the neighbors.

We were all in good spirits as we left on the morning of January 1st, 2017. We averaged around 300 miles a day. No need to push it; we could afford to take the time to see the Grand Canyon and other points-of-interest along the way.

Surprisingly, those eight days on the road went smoothly and without any major hiccups. The kids were great companions and helpers; Danica and I were so proud of them.

We arrived on January 8th to our new house where a volunteer crew was waiting for us. This crew was comprised of parishioners from the church that was renting our building. The previous owner had renters who had access to the building for their Sunday and Wednesday evening services. This was yet another opportunity to encourage Jake and the others regarding how our Heavenly Father was taking care of us so well.

We had a good time of fellowship with the crew as they helped us move in. One thing we thought was funny: They thanked us for our prayers for a mild winter! God was gracious in that regard too.

Before we knew it, we were all settled in and gearing up for the mission at hand.

On Mission

My dad just donated a church property to our non-profit. I thought, what's holding me back from rolling up my sleeves and getting the word out about starting a new church? It's January and Easter is around the corner. Why not go for it?

So, I designed and launched a website. (By the way, check it out at NewVintageWI.org.) I joined the Chamber of Commerce and began attending their meetings. I also joined the local chapter of the Harley-Davidson motorcycle club. I submitted an article about how we ended up in West Allis in the Christian newspaper that they took to print. I put out a Facebook ad, installed new signage on the property, went door-to-door to hand out invitations… Oh, that reminds me of a cool story.

One day while I was at the church I noticed that the boiler-heater system was not working. Not good, especially because we were having our first practice service that Sunday. I didn't want to call my dad and ask for the funds to repair the boiler, so I prayed instead.

"Lord, will You miraculously provide for the funds

to fix this thing? As You know, we have our first service this Sunday, and no one's going to want to stick around once they realize that the boiler isn't working."

"But Lord, I'm going to give You forty-eight hours to provide. After that, I'm just going to assume that You'll provide through my dad. The thing is, though, that I'd rather You provide through some other means so that I can tell my dad how Your miraculous hand of provision came through for me."

When I think back on that prayer, I shudder a little because it wasn't the most reverent one.

After my prayer time at the church I printed up my hundred church invites for the day and headed out to go door-to-door.

There was this one house that I'll never forget. I rang the doorbell. No answer. So, I left an invite on the porch, turned around and started walking down the sidewalk to the next house. Then, I heard the door open and I turned around.

"Hey, how ya doin'? Whatcha got for me?"

"Hi, I'm Paul. I'm a new neighbor of yours. My family and I just moved here from out-of-state and I wanted to introduce myself and give you an invitation to our new Christian church."

"Oh, that's interesting. Nice to meet you, I'm Chad. Where'd you move from?"

"San Diego, California."

"WHAT?! AND YOU MOVED HERE?!"

At this point in the conversation I would share the story of how my family and I ended up here in West Allis. Then, Chad asked how I like the church property.

"I like it a lot, thanks. Well, except for the boiler. I found out this morning that it broke."

Chad then took out his cell phone and began texting someone. "I have a good friend who happens to be a boiler technician. Let's see if he's available right now."

"Right now?"

"Sure, why not? You have anything going on at the moment?"

"Nothing that I can't get back to later."

I heard Chad's phone chirp at him indicating a text received. "Justin's on his way. Once he gets here, we'll hop in his car and get that boiler fixed for you. Sound good?"

"Sure, good times, man!" This day was turning into quite the adventure.

Chad, Justin, and I headed out to the church and Justin looked at the boiler while I showed Chad around. It wasn't too long before Justin was through with his inspection.

"It'll take a few hours and it'll cost you around $60 for the parts. Labors' on me."

"Excuse me?"

"Pastor, I'm not charging you for the labor. This is the first of my many contributions towards your new church. When does service start this Sunday?"

Awesome. God is awesome.

Sunday rolled around and our first practice service went well. It was great to meet Justin's wife and Chad's family.

Soon thereafter, Justin introduced me to a friend of his named Mark. Mark and his wife Patty started attending faithfully, along with one of Lily's friends from school and her family. A neighbor noticed our sign in front of the building and began attending, and another discovered us through the article in the newspaper. It looked like we were going to have a great Easter service.

Easter came and went, and a good time was had by all. This season marked not only our first Easter, but also many other "firsts" for our new church. First time officiating a wedding and first time conducting a funeral. First baptismal service and first membership class. God was on the move.

Where We're at and Where We're Going

(August of 2018)

As you can imagine, when we first arrived to West Allis it was a tough adjustment. As of present though, everyone has found their groove and is doing well. Danica is quite busy as a wife, mom, minister, Home Depot employee, and artist who creates designs for a batik textile company. I started building a freelance copywriting business on the side. The kiddos are doing great in school and have made new friends. They also have become quite the ministers themselves as they work in the multi-media booth and play on the worship team.

Our church has been blessed with the means to provide a quality Sunday morning experience. We've also been blessed with a caring and fun children's church director. We have a vibrant small group ministry and other ministries as well.

Our staff began discussing plans regarding opening a second service to accommodate the growth we're experiencing, and our sanctuary is much bigger than the one we had back in the day, thank goodness.

This reminds me of the Latin phrase *Deo Volente*, which means, "God willing." If God wills it, the church will continue to grow and make a significant impact in the community and at-large.

But what's it all for?

Well, to elaborate, it's about making a significant impact for God's Kingdom, a kingdom of "righteousness, peace, and joy in the Holy Spirit," to borrow the apostle Paul's words. This takes place in the hearts and minds of people who have not yet experienced the freedom made available through being a disciple of Jesus.

But still…

Why all the blood, sweat, and tears? All the sacrifice? Why not just coast through life and eventually retire, grow old and die?

In my most difficult moments I'll catch myself looking back at that little house Danica and I used to own in Oceanside, California. We would have been much closer to having it paid off by now. And then I realize, yet again, that I would have been the most miserable guy on the planet.

That's not the life of a disciple of Jesus. Besides, life is but "a vapor that that appears for a little while and then vanishes," to borrow words from the book of James, so I think I'll keep making my life count for God's Kingdom, for eternity.

How about you?

*"He is no fool who gives what he cannot
keep to gain what he cannot lose."*
~ Philip James Elliott, one of five missionaries killed
while participating in Operation Auca, an attempt
to evangelize the Huaorani people of Ecuador ~

*"Whoever wants to be my disciple must deny themselves
and take up their cross daily and follow me. For whoever
wants to save their life will lose it, but whoever loses
their life for me will find it. What good will it be for
someone to gain the whole world, yet forfeit their soul?
Or what can anyone give in exchange for their soul?"*
~ Jesus, God-incarnate, to His disciples
throughout all of time ~

"Salvation is free, but discipleship costs everything we have."
~ Billy Graham, evangelist for six decades,
estimated lifetime audience of 2.2 billion people,
spiritual advisor to Presidents, and activist ~

*"When Christ calls a man, he bids him come and die…
Discipleship is not an offer that man makes to Christ."*
~ Dietrich Bonhoeffer, who dared to criticize
politicized cultural Christianity and the
Nazi subjugation of churches. He was
executed at the Flossenburg concentration
camp just before its liberation ~

Dear reader, I was blessed to receive the below artwork all the way from Ghana, Africa that I wanted to share with you. These came from some of the children of Promise Land Ranch School, of course. I hope they bring a smile to your face!

Thank you to Acquaye Herbert, Elijah Botchway Tetteh, Edmond Awuley Botchway, Kelvin Nii Okai Tagoe, Solomon Nartey Tetteh, and Kelvin Lomo-Tetteh for your contribution of art for this book.

Dear reader, to play a role in transforming these childrens' lives for the glory of God is indescribable. I pray that God will take both my contribution and yours (by purchasing this book) and multiply it greatly.

- Pastor Paul

Imagine... living in a village in a region of the world where you have no hope for your children to receive an education. Rather, your only hope is that they'll work for their father who has a fishing business. He is only able to provide one meal a day.

A private Christian school opens, and you find out that it's free, unlike the government-run schools. Since your children represent the poorest-of-the-poor, they're selected to become students. They're hungry, and not just for food. They're hungry for an education.

They walk literally 4 miles a day (one way) to class, and they are so excited! Yet, they're gnawing on their pencil erasers to fill their tummy with something... anything.

The school responds by providing nutritious meals, clean water, and even health care. More donors from America provide the funds to purchase a bus. More funds provide for the construction of classroom buildings.

A generation's prayers are answered, and a region begins a transformation for the sake of the Gospel.

Thank you... for purchasing this book and making a difference in the lives of the students of Promise Land Ranch School.

There're more blessings to be had though... for you. "It's more blessed to give than to receive."

Now, it's time... to take this to the next level by visiting the school's website at *https://www.plrghanaafrica.com/* and sponsoring a child today.

Printed in the United States
By Bookmasters